This Book Belongs to:

_____

I am ready to do the WRITE thing!

DO THE Write thing TODAY

 *Reasons to Pen, Polish and Publish your story!*

HILETTE A. VIRGO

Copyright © 2024 Hilette A. Virgo. All rights reserved.

All rights reserved. No portion of this book may be reproduced, stored in a retrieval system, or transmitted in any form or by any means – electronic, mechanical, photocopy, recording, scanning, or other – except for a brief quotation in critical reviews or articles, without the prior written permission of the publisher or author.

Published by:

Cover designed by Calbert Simpson

Table of Contents

Introduction 7

Acknowledgment 10

Chapter 1: Write to Heal and Liberate Yourself 14

Chapter 2: Writing to Honor God 30

Chapter 3: Write to Inspire and Save a Soul 44

Chapter 4: Writing Enlarges your Influence
and Help you Reach Many People 56

Chapter 5: Writing a Book Helps to Raise Your
Self-Esteem and Confidence 67

Chapter 6: Write Because Your Story is Unique 79

Chapter 7: Write to Leave a Legacy 88

Conclusion 98

About the Author 100

"Publish His glorious deeds among the nations. Tell everyone about the amazing things He does."
1 Chronicles 16:24 (NLT)

Introduction

"Fill your paper with the breathings of your heart."
- William Wordsworth

In the tapestry of human emotions, a few threads weave a more intricate and magnificent pattern than the art of writing. In addition to its literary merits, writing possesses a remarkable ability to enable and accelerate healing, build and boost confidence, connect and influence growth and change, bring solace and relief to wounded hearts and minds, and confer mere mortals the lofty honor to glorify and give credence to the Author and Finisher of our faith.

As an editor and book coach, having published numerous memoirs, devotionals, and faith-based books, I have had the profound benefit of witnessing firsthand the awe-inspiring power of penning, polishing, and publishing one's words. I have seen authors gleefully express how refreshed, renewed, and restored they are after embarking on the authorship journey. Many have expressed the life-changing, redemptive power this process has had on their minds and its transformative influence on their lives.

The cathartic chemical combination of ink and tears has repaired many broken hearts, restored many shattered minds, and renewed many exhausted spirits. When God gave me the green light to write, I knew I was not only engaging in an art of self-expression; I knew I was doing the WRITE thing. That write thing changed my life completely, and since then, He has ordained and commissioned me to help and encourage others to do the WRITE thing. This book is a response to that appointment.

It is uniquely written to help you understand, recognize, and embrace the benefits of writing. *Do the Write Thing Today* gained breath from an online presentation on December 3, 2023. The response of the gleeful audience was resounding and encouraging, and many testified that they were stirred and charged up to do the *write* thing. I was, therefore, led to validate and authenticate the message by making it timeless and boundless through publishing.

I pray that the hands, eyes, ears, hearts, and minds that behold this work will be blessed and that its ripples will disseminate to bring light and love to all touched.

Acknowledgment

This work is exceptionally special because of the contribution of both the mortal and the Immortal. The Holy Spirit inspired both the book's content and the authors who were approached and selected for validatory testimonials. All glory goes to the Godhead for the inspiration, wisdom, and knowledge ascribed to pen, polish, and publish this book. I dedicate it as a sacrifice of praise to the One who gave me the gifts of writing, editing, and helping others to birth their literary work. I am thrilled yet humbled to be chosen to release this message through this remarkable channel of influence. Thanks for using me, Lord.

I must recognize the coalition of authors who availed themselves and gave their time and talent and their affirmation and support of the "Doing the WRITE Thing" campaign. Their prompt response and gracious words have blessed me immensely, and I pray these inked symbols and coordinated syllables will be the fuel you need to propel your writing journey. Candice Andrews-Bailey, Ontonio Dawson, Marsha Gregg, Miguel Lowe, Shasta Green, and Angeline Edwards, I am beyond grateful for your love and support. Your contribution to this work is monumental and highly esteemed.

Special thanks and support to Serena Rowe, who was instrumental in helping me organize the content of this book. You are one of the most dedicated and supportive people I know. I couldn't do this without you and our friend Mike. I thank you both for helping me lay the foundation for its successful completion.

I thank Janet Fider for saying yes to sharing how writing has been a blessing to her family through her 96-year-old father's authorship. Although you are not yet an author, I am grateful for your advocacy of doing the WRITE thing. Continue being a supportive and lovely soul.

I thank my team at Great-Nest Publishing Inc., especially Calbert Simpson, for the rich support you give through graphics. I couldn't do what I do without your tireless contribution and support. May God continue to bless you richly.

I thank all my clients, past, present, and future, for trusting me with their messages and allowing me to usher them into authorship. Thank you and continue to Do the WRITE Thing!

"There is no greater agony than bearing an untold story within you."

- Maya Angelou

Chapter 1

Write to Heal and Liberate Yourself

The Healing Power of Words

"Writing is a form of therapy; sometimes I wonder how all those who do not write, ... manage to escape the melancholia, the panic and fear which is inherent in a human situation."
- *Graham Greene.*

Writing is one of the best antidotes for a toxic, broken, and battered spirit. It has the power to invigorate and regulate the mind and set a captive spirit free. Writing is to the emotional and psychological well-being as vitamins to the physical body. Writing, like reading, can boost the immune system of the mind and support mental and emotional growth and development. It also sharpens the brain cells. Many psychologists and therapists recommend writing as a tool for healing as it exercises the brain's hemispheres, stimulates its motor cortex, solidifies memories, and helps keep the mind dexterous.

This chapter delves into the profound ways writing can be a transformative force, aiding in the journey of personal and emotional recovery. It starts with the testimony of Candice, a Trinidadian young lady who has encountered the healing wonders of scripting. Candice did the "write thing" and prescribed it as a tonic, nourishment, and vitamin for anyone looking for a life revolution. She shares briefly how she has accessed immense healing through penning and publishing her story and how it has opened a whole new world for her. I then share some points I have put together through research and firsthand knowledge of how writing facilitates healing.

Dealing with my pain on the Pages

"At this very moment, I'm immensely grateful for where I am presently in life. After being rescued by God, I can finally breathe the fresh air of restoration and feel the cool breeze of renewal. How could someone like me climb out of a dark tunnel of trouble without losing my mind? I did the WRITE thing! This process facilitated a significant shift and stretched me beyond my imagination.

Every time I sit to write, it's a cathartic experience to transfer the experience in my mind to the page. However, sometimes it is a struggle, but I thank God for my editor and book coach, Hilette Virgo, who is equipped with the skills to help me translate my thoughts into a language that readers everywhere can appreciate while encouraging and holding my hand through the process.

My story of authorship came at a time in my life when I felt numb and speechless. I had become withdrawn and quiet but could be loud on the page. I remember taking out my phone while traveling in the local taxi in South Trinidad and making notes on my notes app. Oh, how relieved I felt after every brain dump. Then, one day, a friend sent me a link. The message was about a book coach seeking writers to contribute to an anthology. I always wanted to write a book, but my mindset about writing for public consumption always got in the way. I failed the English language at the Caribbean Secondary Examination Counsel (CSEC) level, which shredded my confidence to shards, so while I was comfortable with journaling on my phone, I thought myself incapable of exposing it to the judgmental eyes of the world.

I loved reading, but it did not help my writing ability. What was in the way? Alas! My emotions and mindset were blocking my confidence and creativity. Additionally, I am an overthinker with a few unruly nerves, constantly insisting that everything must be perfect. However, with my book coach's assistance, I accessed my creativity by knocking down the blockbusters that kept me captive, and I subdued the perfectionist minions that kept me stagnant. I learned my duty was to pen and leave the polishing to my capable book coach and editor. Consequently, writing unlocked a world I never knew existed and took me to heights I never knew I could climb.

In the labyrinth of my life, I found solace and safety through the power of pressing a pen against the page. Most of my writing started on a physical page, and then I transferred it to the blank digital sheets of Microsoft Word. The best way to share the many blessings writing gave me is to break it down like a mother bird crushing worms in small parts to make them easier to digest.

Writing gave me a space to empty my emotions into pages that were strong enough to bear all the things I'd been through.

I call it my therapeutic outlet, my safe and sacred space. There was no judgment, no strange stares or scrutinizing looks. It was easy to see my pain like a five-course spread on a clear table. The page became a clean plate on which I could dish out what I felt at the time. What I'd gone through became palatable as I ladled from my trauma pot, one pain after another. Authorship allowed me to dish out and address my abusive past, face my fears, process my aches, and eventually find a language to interpret my struggles.

I always wondered, when Jesus wrote on the ground, what made the accusers of that woman flee? Did he expose the leaders of the day? Was it a love letter? One finger, touching the sand and forming words, saved a woman from being stoned to death. In like manner, one word followed by another, then another saved and liberated me. The accusatory voice in my head no longer had ammunition to use against me. I no longer had to remain captive to grief, depression, and fear. God cannot pour new wine into old wineskin; He first needs us to expose our experiences and empty them to Him so He can use us effectively. Some people incorporate prayer journals to help them pray. Again, this shows the power of when pen meets paper. However, writing for publication takes the healing to another level. It guided me in beginning the healing process as it positioned me to evaluate my healing journey.

Though I felt dead, writing made me feel alive again.

From writing a chapter in *Waiting in the Pit Vol 1* to writing another in *Waiting in the Pit Vol 2*, sharing my experiences with grief and depression, I grew and gained strength with every publication.

The first anthology was the perfect platform to launch me into the authorship realm. Knowing I was not the only one with a pit story made sharing easier and better. Each book starts with a line, paragraph, page, and chapter; before you know it, you have a book. Contributing to those first two books gave me the confidence, one step at a time, to finally jump out on my own and produce my book. It was a tangible way to record my story of overcoming. When your past is on the page, it brings inner peace and pleasure to your life. It calms and comforts you all at the same time.

What was important to me in that season was that I educated the masses about mental and emotional health. Writing gave me the authority to address and edify the church's community on ways to navigate and handle grief and depression. Writing was my way of addressing issues I couldn't verbalize with my mouth, and it gave me an outlet to make peace with them.

When the page speaks for you, it does a better job because it's not enslaved by peer pressure or pain.

After writing, I no longer felt paralyzed; I now felt purposeful. The process felt like I was helping someone other than myself climb out of numerous pits. I was helping them process what they had been trying to push past for years and break down stigmas.

It has been quite a journey. While preparing for my first taste of authorship in *Waiting in the Pit Vol 1*, I was in a relationship. In this anthology, I dealt with (for the first time) my emotions concerning my father's death when I was only eight years old. Writing about it was painful, and I had to be induced several times by my coach to release it finally. I breathed a sigh of relief after carrying this burden for over twenty years. During this time, I was courting a ministerial student whose life's goal and mission aligned with mine. This "new thing" God was doing looked promising, and we were leaning toward marriage. By the time the book was published, my fiancé died suddenly of a heart attack. He was only 33 years old. The death transported me to another silent place. It rocked my world.

After losing the man I thought God prepared for me, I was a hunched-back woman with camel humps of unspoken grief. Then, I remembered what writing did for me. I can safely say writing was the right thing to do. It helped me to navigate the dance between death and depression. Pouring it all on the page is an unexplainable occurrence. The blank feeling of being bombarded by emotional bruises birthed my book, *The stretched-out Life*. It was born out of sorrow, but God did not leave me in the quicksand of sadness.

My coach encouraged me to write again, so I contributed to the second anthology, *Waiting in the Pit*. It wasn't easy because I had a timeline, and my grief still tormented me.

Before the book could be published, guess what happened? It opened the path to another promise God had for me. He promised to restore, but I didn't think He would do it so quickly (in less than a year). Writing became part of my pivoting plan. Every time I wrote, it cleared the path for God to release a new blessing. Once I released my message, the man God had in store for me appeared.

Writing paved the way for God to present one of His favored sons to me. The writing process ensured I addressed the adverse storm within so God could entrust me with the beautiful complexities of a relationship that resulted in marriage. Today, my husband walks around with a copy of my book and uses it as a talking point to evangelize or capture a sale on my behalf. As I write this contribution, I confess I am happily married. Writing, in all its exciting essence, became a conduit for divine intervention and restoration for me.

Writing helped me see weakness as a weapon.

Each writing experience became a testament to my strength, resilience, and personal growth. Penning my past became an ally in my journey towards achieving some of my most significant accomplishments. Once again, writing has come to save the day because while writing this testimony, I have another tab opened as I am writing the life story of my late fiancé to honor his memory as he has made an indelible contribution to mission and ministry. Writing this testimony gives me the impetus and inspires me to complete it. Writing seems to be my healing strategy.

The day I was invited to write was not just an invitation to put words on a Word document but an invitation to a better life. It was a companion, a guide, a friend, a brain cooler, a path to self-discovery, healing, and ultimately, the life God meant for me to live.

Writing words gave me a new voice, a new narrative of strength.

I invite you to a better life, the author's life.

Please activate the content of this book and do the write thing today! I pray you trust God to give you the strength to face the page and produce your story. Don't miss your opportunity to open a new door, to be restored, transformed, and healed. Please reach out to the author of this book or a book coach and "Do the write thing today!""

Candice Andrews-Bailey
Author: The Stretched-out Life
Teacher
Visibility Coach

"The Process of writing a book has given me a whole new reverence for writers. Mechanically, it is a brutal process, emotionally, it's incredibly healing."
- Cory Booker

As you have pored over Candice's testimony, I know you are already enlightened tangibly about how penning and polishing one's piece can be healing and restorative. However, here are some other points to show how it promotes the therapeutic and healing process:

1. **Self-Reflection and Expression:** Writing for publishing provides a unique avenue for self-reflection and expression. While journaling is an effective channel to reflect and express inner emotions and thoughts, writing with an audience in mind challenges the writer to be more organized, thorough, and creative with their expressions. It

helps the writer reach deeper, wider, and higher in the sanctuary of their mind to extract remarkable treasures.

When faced with emotional turmoil, putting pen to paper or fingers to keyboard allows individuals to articulate their thoughts and feelings. This expression can be a powerful step towards understanding, acknowledging, and healing from emotional wounds. Penning a story or journey allows the writer to analyze their emotions and gain deeper insight into one's experiences and personality, facilitating a deeper connection with themselves.

2. **Release of Pent-Up Emotions:** Bottling up emotions can be detrimental to mental well-being. Writing serves as a constructive channel for releasing these pent-up feelings. Individuals can unburden their hearts and minds through poetry or prose, freeing themselves from the weight of unresolved emotions.

3. **Creating a Narrative of Healing:** Writing enables individuals to craft a narrative of their healing journey. By documenting experiences, challenges, and triumphs in an organized and structured

manner, individuals can witness their evolution over time. This process fosters a sense of accomplishment and provides a tangible record of resilience and growth that others can witness and benefit from. It helps the writer to shift from seeing themselves as the victor rather than the victim. The memoir *I See God* readily comes to mind. Angela Nichol, after sharing her journey of renal failure, although still ill, could refocus her attention from her illness after she wrote her book. She could see herself as a strong source of inspiration and resiliency for the first time. This helped her overcome feelings of depression.

4. **Gaining Perspective:** When faced with emotional distress, perspectives can become skewed. Writing allows individuals to step back, gain a more objective view of their experiences, and assess how renewed and relieved they feel after they have penned their stories and released them in the sea of authorship. It becomes a tool for examining situations from different angles, fostering a more profound understanding essential for healing.

5. **Empowerment through Creativity:** Writing creatively can be an empowering experience. Crafting stories, poems, or even fictionalized accounts of personal experiences allows individuals to reclaim a sense of authority. Through the creative process, writers become the designers of their stories, shaping the course of their healing journey. Sharing this process with others makes it even more profound. It's like getting an extra boost of tonic or vitamins.

6. **Connection with Others:** Writing can connect people on a profound level. Sharing one's writing in a book creates a sense of community. The reviews, testimonials, and feedback boost your mental health as they trigger the feel-good chemicals (endorphins and serotonin) that can decrease stress and anxiety. Also, knowing that others have faced similar struggles and triumphed can be a source of inspiration and encouragement.

7. **Mindfulness and Presence:** Writing encourages mindfulness, anchoring individuals in the present moment. Writing a book fosters a level of

concentration and commitment to the task that is good for brain power. The creation of expressive art through writing draws attention to the now, fostering a sense of presence that is crucial for healing.

Written words testify to the resilience of the human spirit in the realm of healing. Through self-expression, reflection, narrative creation, connecting with an audience, practicing mindfulness, gaining perspectives, and releasing pent-up emotions, writing becomes a guiding companion on the path to recovery.

May the pen be a tool of healing in the chapters of our lives, rewriting stories of pain into stories of strength, resilience, and renewal. Heal your mind, heal your soul. Do the WRITE thing today! Pen, Polish, and Publish your story.

"Worship is the proper response of all moral, sentient beings to God, ascribing all honor and worth to their Creator—God precisely because He is worthy, delightfully so."
- D. A. Carson

Chapter 2

Writing to Honor God

Writing is a Form of Worship

This shall be written for the generations to come: and the people which shall be created shall praise the Lord.
(Psalms 102:18)

Writing is one of the most beautiful forms of worship. After all, God Himself is the first Author. In His infinite wisdom, He conceptualized this phenomenon and invited men to join Him on this noble course. Outside of the Bible, God has His documentation of life. The Bible declares that God authors multiple books. "And I saw the dead, small and great, stand before God; and the books were opened: and another book was opened, which is the book of life: and the dead were judged out of those things which were written in the books, according to their works." (Revelation 20:12) The "Book of Life" is referenced several times in Scripture and is described as the record book that captures the names of every human being that was conceived. It is timeless and has been around from the foundation of the world (Revelation 13:8, 17:8).

Additionally, Psalm 139:15-16 tells us that from the moment we were conceived, God documented a design for each part of our bodies in a book and outlined how He planned to fashion us in it. He established writing from the foundation of the world as a powerful and impactful way to preserve knowledge, communicate, and establish authority. As God's crowned creation, made in His image, God extended an invitation for humankind to do the *write* thing and document our experiences and other critical aspects of life. He called, chose, and trained us to write words that have been the most significant source of healing, comfort, and edification.

From time immemorial, the written word has been a cornerstone and bedrock for humankind. God used it as a vehicle to communicate His love, precepts, and commands and preserve history. He has also given us a glimpse of His character through His word.

Noteworthily, the Bible is the world's most printed, translated, and sold book and has the most significant influence and power. The Guinness World Records confirmed that it is the best-selling book of all time, selling over five billion copies. Naturally, it is also the world's most translated book. The Author of languages, through the incredible power of the Holy Spirit, inspired and directed men across 195 countries to translate and circulate His word. The complete Bible has been translated into almost 700 languages, and specific parts have been converted to over 3,300 of the world's 7,139 languages (according to the Ethnologue Guide). This shows how much God values His word and the art of writing.

Writing is an act of worship because it is a response to God's directive. All the authors in the Bible wrote in response to the beckoning of the Holy Spirit. God calls His people to write because when we write, we remember. He calls us to remember His precepts and laws, where He has taken us from, that He is sovereign, to recognize Him as Creator, to remember His promises, kindness, and redemptive works, and to behold His testimonies and prophecies. His words have been a guidepost for humanity to live a complete and wholesome life. It is the most beautiful literary work and has inspired millions to claim the prolific power of the pen and document their journey for publication.

There are several places in the Bible where God called His people to write:

In Deuteronomy 17:18-20 God commands a king to write his copy of God's law in a book: "It is to be with him, and he is to read it all the days of his life so that he may learn to revere the Lord his God and follow carefully all the words of this law and these decrees **20** and not consider himself better than his fellow Israelites and turn from the law to the right or to the left. Then he and his descendants will reign a long time over his kingdom in Israel." (NIV)

In Habakuk 2:2, the Lord disclosed a revelation to His prophet, Habakkuk. He gives the directive: "Write the vision And make it plain on tablets, That he may run who reads it." (NKJV)

God also spoke to Jeremiah directly, telling him to "Write in a book all the words I have spoken to you." (Jeremiah 30:2 NIV)

God is still giving His people visions and testimonies to share. Like the king in Deuteronomy 17, He instructs us to write books that highlight His word and detail our experiences with Him. He wants us to write books that introduce, exalt, and draw people to Him and testify of His workings in our lives. Writing is a noble expedition, and we honor God when we write what He has placed on our hearts and script materials that will benefit humanity.

As a faith-based publisher, I have seen countless authors dedicate their work to the honor and glory of God. Many were anxious initially when the Holy Spirit instructed them to share painful elements of their lives or past, but as they pressed through and completed their work, they felt a sense of peace, as if heaven approved of their effort.

Marsha is a native of Bequia, the largest island in St. Vincent and the Grenadines. She embarked on a writing journey after suffering several painful experiences in her past. Writing became the avenue through which she accessed healing and developed a stronger relationship with God.

She shares her experience of how her life transformed after she accepted and embraced the call to do the *write* thing!

"Surreal! That's the word I use to describe this moment. I am at a juncture where I can look back over my life's journey with a smile. There are still painful moments, but the restorative power of God is real, and we all experience it differently. I experienced it through writing; in other words, I did the WRITE thing.

I started writing very young because I found it to be my safe place. After enduring multiple sexual abuse, my freedom came through pen and paper. I poured on the pages the feelings of insecurity, hate, anger, low self-esteem, and poor self-image I experienced. I wrote as a way of escape and not to become a published author.

Over the years, I accumulated many journals and started scripting my story on any surface firm enough to bear my pain. This became a deeply personal and reflective practice. I found a connection between my words and my inner spirit. It was like a sacred communion expressed through my words. Writing became the channel through which I explored who I was, and though there were moments when reality became too much to embrace, I still pressed on, understanding that the benefits of release were great.

I developed the desire to write my book but had no idea where to start, coupled with the effects of imposter syndrome, asking myself, "Who do I think I am to write my story?" and "What made me think I can publish it for the world?" While scrolling through Facebook, I noticed one of my friends expressing gratitude to her book coach for guiding her through publishing her book. Without a second thought, I contacted the book coach, and about a month or so later, we were planning my book. I felt the heaviness of inadequacy lifted as I embraced my coach's faith in my story, knowing I didn't have to be the expert because my book coach made the process easier.

As I delved into the writing process, I felt a sense of surrender, an acknowledgment that the words were imperfect vessels attempting to convey the inexpressible. Writing became my meditation because it was a way to silence the external noise and attune myself to the divine frequency. It was not merely a means of communication but a way to transcend the limitations of my imperfect world. Writing became a sacred endeavor to me; every word became a prayer, each sentence a hymn. My pen was transformed into a holy instrument, and the blank page into a canvas for divine expression. Writing became a journey into my soul, a quest to unveil its mysteries and connect into spaces I was once afraid to enter.

As I embarked on the sacred pilgrimage of reliving my story in the pages of my book, *The Divinely Orchestrated Woman*, I found peace in seeing how God's love was intertwined with my various experiences.

As I navigated the maze of my thoughts, emotions, and experiences, each pen stroke became a rhythm that resonated with the heartbeat of who I was created to be.

Writing has opened the floodgates of possibilities for me. I have been invited to speak on various platforms in women's empowerment programs, and this has propelled me to launch my podcast, named after my book, as a medium for women to share their stories and create a more significant impact in our community and worldwide. While writing this testimony, I'm also outlining a biography of my pastor. I never believed I could write for the world; however, having gone through the process, I found it's one of my treasured gifts.

DO THE WRITE THING TODAY

Writing has been and still is a means of self-discovery and self-transcendence. I am not merely a narrator but a pilgrim on a journey of my soul. Through articulating my innermost thoughts, I confronted my vulnerabilities, grappled with doubts, and celebrated profound insight and victory moments. Writing became a vessel for my transformation.

I implore you to do the WRITE thing. Engage fully in the process and experience its power to heal, inspire, illuminate your path, and draw you closer to God. Through writing, the mundane details of life are transmuted into sacred narratives, and ordinary moments become portals to God.

As you partake of the contents of this book, I pray the insights you receive will fuel you to start your writing journey. Ignore the voice of doubts, imposter syndrome, fear, or anxiety and do the *write* thing. If you feel a tug on your heart, that's the Holy Spirit beckoning. Let this be your invitation to embark on a journey of self-discovery and a celebration of the infinite possibilities that unfold when you partner with God and do the *write* thing."

Marsha Gregg
Founder and CEO of Thrives Inc.
Author, speaker, financial coach

Sharing your testimony can glorify God in several profound ways:

1. **Acknowledging God's Transformative Power:** Your testimony is a living testament to the transformative power of God. By openly sharing your personal experiences, struggles, and the positive changes God has wrought in your life, you acknowledge His ability to bring about meaningful transformation.

2. **Inspiring Others:** Your story has the potential to inspire and uplift others who may be going through similar challenges. As you share how God has been a source of strength, hope, and restoration in your life, you become a living testimony of His grace, offering encouragement to those in need.

3. **Reflecting God's Faithfulness:** When you share your testimony, you highlight God's faithfulness throughout your journey. Even amid trials, setbacks, and uncertainties, your narrative becomes a testament to God's unwavering presence and His commitment to walking alongside His children.

4. **Demonstrating God's Love and Mercy:** A testimony often includes moments of redemption, forgiveness, and grace. By sharing how God has extended His love and mercy to you, you reflect the core tenets of Christianity. Your testimony becomes a living example of God's boundless love, forgiveness, and willingness to embrace His children.

5. **Bringing Glory to God's Name:** As you recount the chapters of your life where God intervened, provided, and guided, you bring glory to His name. Your testimony becomes a praise report, magnifying God's sovereignty, wisdom, and goodness.

6. **Encouraging Authenticity in Faith:** Authenticity is a powerful aspect of a testimony. By openly sharing both the highs and lows of your spiritual journey, you encourage authenticity in others. This transparency fosters a genuine connection within the faith community and underscores the reality that everyone, regardless of their spiritual maturity, is a work in progress.

7. **Strengthening Your Own Faith:** The act of sharing your testimony is not only for the benefit of others but also for your spiritual growth. As you vocalize your experiences, you reinforce your dependence on God and deepen your understanding of His role in your life. This process strengthens your faith and commitment to God.

8. **Fostering Gratitude:** A testimony often involves reflecting on the blessings, answered prayers, and moments of divine intervention. The authors of the Psalms give powerful evidence of this. Their words of gratitude resonate with millions who in return used them to echo their gratefulness. By expressing gratitude for God's goodness, provision, and guidance, you cultivate a heart of thanksgiving, acknowledging that every good and perfect gift comes from Him.

In essence, sharing your testimony is a powerful way to glorify God by proclaiming His work in your life, inspiring others, and reinforcing the foundational truths of the Christian faith. When you share your story, it becomes a testament to the ongoing narrative of God's love, grace, and transformative power in the lives of His people. Do the write thing today and share your testimony in a polished, published work and use it to honor God.

"...Therefore every scribe which is instructed unto the kingdom of heaven is like unto a man that is a householder, which bringeth forth out of his treasure things new and old."
(Matthew 13:52 KJV)

Chapter 3

Write to Inspire and Save a Soul

"Publish his glorious deeds among the nations. Tell everyone about the amazing things he does."
(1 Chronicles 16:24 NLT)

Your past hurts, sorrows, grief, deliverance, and victory stories could be the rope of hope someone needs to pull them from the depths of life's pits. When we write our stories and share messages God gave us, we extend ourselves as missionaries to save lost, broken souls. You never know how the Holy Spirit will lead someone who has gone through or is going through similar events that you have encountered to read your story and be convicted of giving their lives to God.

Many have testified that a book, outside God's holy words, has brought them to Christ. I have benefited from many memoirs, devotionals, and inspirational pieces when I experienced moments of gloom. One of my favorite books is Roger Morneau's *The Incredible Power of Prayer*. I have read this book several times as I am intrigued by the testimonies shared by a man who once worshiped the enemy of the soul. To know that God can restore, redeem, and elevate someone to a level where they have tapped into a colossal heavenly source that he sees his prayers answered incredibly in record time inspires me to press into God's presence on a deeper level.

Many other books by countless authors have drawn me closer to God and helped me love and appreciate Him more. Ellen G. White's *Steps to Christ* is another of my favorites, and it has helped me experience Christ on an intimate level.

Jesus Himself used writing as a soul-saving tool. When He stooped down and wrote on the ground, as documented in John 8:1-11, His act of writing not only saved the woman "caught" in the act of adultery from the fury of her accusers, but it saved her soul. Jesus did the *write* thing in this profound moment and pacified a crowd that was determined to sentence her to death. Jesus' stooping and writing was an invitation to us to write our stories of pain and shame to release us from condemnation, guilt, and contempt. When you own and acknowledge your shortcomings and repent of them, the enemy has no ammunition to use against you. Documenting it in a book in ink is like signing your contract of freedom, especially when you share how you have been delivered and redeemed from the besetting sin or experience.

One of my readers testified how she shared my first book, *Activating Her Eagle Instincts*, with a friend who was contemplating suicide. The friend related that my book lifted her spirit and ushered her to a better mindset and appreciation of self because of the Scriptures and affirmations I wrote, reminding my readers how much God valued them. Many of my clients have also shared testimonials of readers who told them that their book was precisely what they needed during tough times. Angeline Edwards, author of *GET Ready! For the Promise* blesses us with her testimony of how she uses her story as a tool for soul-winning.

"I had to develop the courage to get outside of myself. I needed to make changes within and get comfortable being uncomfortable with the process I was experiencing at the beckoning of the Holy Spirit. After enduring years of heartache, sorrow, and grief, it was time to make those years of gloom count. I could feel that I was approaching my years of bloom. However, I needed to yield wholly to the Holy Spirit, obey the call, and follow God's directive. Little did I know that this entailed Him ushering me to a higher level in my walk.

I spent years pouring out my emotions and pain through poetic channels, and the experience was thrilling. However, I did not see how transformative and impactful writing for publishing in a book was until I wrote a chapter in *Waiting in the Pit Vol 1* anthology. I grew up in a ministerial family where my dad was a pastor, and ministry was the center of our life. I preached and served in various capacities in my church and spearheaded several ministries. I understood what it meant to save souls for the kingdom of God but never imagined that writing and sharing my story in a published work could accomplish that in such a remarkable and profound way.

During the writing process, I learned quickly that my challenges were not about me. Even though I went through them, they were for God's glory and to reach others. Writing, I realized, was one of the most effective routes to relate my experiences and connect meaningfully with diverse audiences. By writing, I received healing, developed an unprecedented confidence boost, and realized it was a great way to reach souls for the kingdom of God.

I experienced peace and great satisfaction knowing that the testimony I shared in the mentioned book touched people worldwide, and many were blessed with what I shared. Though delighted to be a part of such a remarkable cohort of co-authors, I was not satisfied. I had a burning desire to share my whole story. Thus, I embarked on a journey to pour everything I had with the primary purpose of impacting and saving souls. If my book was the seed that could be watered in a reader's heart to usher them into the kingdom, that was enough for me.

I couldn't stop writing the moment I started. The book was completed in less than three months, and when I wrote the last word, I tasted tears that had a different flavor. My bitter tears now had a savory taste. When I realized that my mess had transformed into an entire message and a ministry and that all my tests had become a testimony, I couldn't hold back the gushing spring of joy in my eyes. I am an overcomer and am in awe that God is willing to use my imperfect life and story remarkably.

I am proud to declare that I now serve people through my writing. By writing, I am holding other people's hands, helping them through what I have gone through, and reassuring my kindreds in spirit that they are not alone. If I survived all that came to kill me, so can they.

Writers are healers following God's example because God has a book. He is the first Author, inspiring 40 people to write His book. Therefore, we are modeling God to write our testimony. We collaborate with Christ when we accept the call to be an author.

My life's goal is to inspire, uplift, instruct, and tell people the lessons I've learned and what I've implemented so that they can learn lessons and don't have to make the mistakes I made.

Writing freed me. I was like a bird released from a cage. I have gotten the opportunity to tell my story my way, and I am thrilled that I will not go to my grave and be buried with it. Once you write, it liberates you, and the opportunities are endless as God rewards the diligent work you put into writing and blesses others.

My life is a testimony of how Jesus worked in, with, and through me. There are many ways to testify and witness, but writing books is a higher level of reaching people, inspiring, and setting captives free. I will continue to write and share with others how God has worked in my life. I invite you to join the throng of soul-savers and do the *write* thing today."

Angeline Edwards
Life Coach,
Author
Motivational Speaker

One soul is waiting desperately for your story to heal and set it free. Share your story and proclaim what God has done for you, knowing that your testimony can inspire and save a soul in several impactful ways:

1. **Relatability:** When you share your testimony, others may find elements of their struggles, doubts, or experiences mirrored in your story. This relatability creates a connection, making it easier for individuals to see that they are not alone in their journey.

2. **Demonstrating God's Power:** Your testimony is a powerful narrative of God's transformative work in your life. By sharing how God has brought healing, restoration, or positive change, you demonstrate His power to save and transform. This can inspire hope and faith in others who may be seeking answers.

3. **Highlighting God's Love and Grace:** The love and grace of God are often central themes in a testimony. As you recount moments of forgiveness, redemption, and unconditional love, you portray a God who is not only powerful but also compassionate. This depiction can resonate deeply with those searching for love and meaning.

4. **Emphasizing the Role of Faith:** Your testimony provides a tangible example of faith in action. By

sharing how your faith in God sustained you through challenges, guided your decisions, and brought you closer to Him, you illustrate the transformative power of a genuine relationship with God.

5. **Addressing Doubts and Questions:** Many individuals grapple with doubts and questions about faith. Your testimony can address these uncertainties by sharing how you navigated your doubts and found answers in your relationship with God. This openness can help others on their journey of faith.

6. **Encouraging Personal Reflection:** Hearing someone else's testimony often prompts individuals to reflect on their own lives, beliefs, and spiritual condition. Your story may catalyze self-examination, leading individuals to consider their need for God's saving grace.

7. **Inspiring a Desire for Change:** When your testimony includes a positive transformation or a turning point, it can inspire a desire for change in others. People may recognize areas in their own

lives where change is needed, and your story can motivate them to seek God's guidance for transformation.

8. **Sharing the Gospel Message:** Your testimony naturally becomes a platform to share the core message of the gospel—the good news of salvation through Jesus Christ. As you recount how God has worked in your life, you have the opportunity to convey the central message of God's love, Christ's sacrifice, and the invitation to accept Him as Lord and Savior.

9. **Offering a Testimonial Invitation:** By openly sharing your testimony, you extend an invitation for others to explore faith and experience God's saving grace. Your story becomes an invitation for others to embark on their journey of faith and discover the life-changing power of a relationship with Christ.

Remember that the impact of your testimony may extend beyond what you can immediately see or measure. You never know how God will choose to use your story to bless countless souls. The Holy Spirit can use your story to work in the hearts of those who hear it, drawing them closer to

God and leading them to a saving knowledge of Jesus Christ. Partner with your heavenly father in missions and ministry, and use your testimony as a soul-saving tool.

"We write to taste life twice, in the moment and in retrospect."

*- **Anais Nin***

Chapter 4

Writing Enlarges your Influence and Help you Reach Many People

"If you want to change the world, pick up your pen and write."
- *Martin Luther*

I've shared countlessly how penning, polishing, and publishing my first book opened doors of opportunities for mission and impact I never knew possible. Writing gave my ministry wings. I have lost count of the number of countries my books have perched. Not only has it enlarged my scope of influence, but it has impacted my life in ways inexpressible.

I have made connections through my books and met people I wouldn't have met under normal circumstances. While you may have a platform or community of people you interact with in your job, church, family circle, or on social media, writing and publishing have the potential to reach places and impact people most profoundly. I have heard authors from all walks of life speak of the ocean of opportunities a book has created for them. While videos, memes, and messages may go viral quickly on the internet, because of the microwave culture, content expires quickly. A well-written book, however, captures more extensive and meaningful messages and doesn't have a limited shelf life.

I love to remind my clients that their books will outlive them. Notwithstanding, the possible benefits that you can derive are endless. A book gives you authority and credibility. Through properly polished work, you can become the person in your field that people go to for solutions or trust as a dependable source. No one has your story; no matter how similar someone else's story, your story furnishes you as an authentic source.

Ontonio Dawson, author of *God's Seed for Success,* shares how writing has enlarged his influence and helped him to reach scores of people globally:

"In the beginning was the Word, the Word was with God, and the Word was God (John 1:1). God used words to create the world and has allowed everyone to use words to create a life of purpose. Words are powerful; they can create or kill. Everyone has a story or stories to tell, and there is no better way to share your story for maximum impact than to write the words of wisdom God has placed in your heart in a book. Books are transgenerational resources that never die and have the capacity to inspire, encourage, and transform lives.

In 2020, with the support and motivation of my dear friend Hilette Virgo, I was able to publish my first book, *God's Seed for Success.* When the idea to write this book was conceived, I knew I had a message to share but had no clue how it would impact people. One of the most mind-blowing experiences I had after writing my book was receiving a message from a young man who was incarcerated. He had received a copy from a friend. He expressed how the book changed his mindset and gave him tools to transform his life from drought to growth. He noted that he felt hopeless before receiving the book, but reading it reminded him that he is God's seed for success. He could see beyond the darkness he was experiencing and focus on the light within him—Jesus. He reconnected with his faith in God, and we have kept in touch ever since. The last time we spoke, he was getting ready to take his freedom and walk out of prison. He plans to write his own story and publish it in a book. My book helped him to be optimistic about living a transformed life and serving Jesus and the community.

Additionally, my book has reached people in parts of the world I have never traveled to and may never get the opportunity to travel. It's incredible to know that a book can reach people who seem unreachable and change people who appear unchangeable. A book can become the wings you never had and take you places you had no dream of reaching. Writing a book allows you to become an expert in a subject matter, and integrating my psychological and theological knowledge in my book gave me the privilege to speak on various platforms using a psychospiritual approach. It has given me credibility and confidence when

I step on any platform to encourage, motivate, or transform lives.

Furthermore, I am constantly inspired by the testimonies of others the book has reached. The feedback I receive often inspires me daily and ignites a fire to never stop reaching for greatness and touching lives. One lady who struggles with her mental health and sleep deprivation left a comment saying, *"When I wake up in the middle of the night feeling troubled, reading this, I can go straight back to sleep feeling the worry lift from me."* It's humbling to know that God has blessed me with words of wisdom that can bring someone peace in hard times.

Another person sent me a message to say, *"I was going through a period of darkness, and I must tell you that I heard a voice say, 'Remember that book that you purchased, God's Seed for Success? read it.' When I read this book, I was so motivated by its content. I was reminded of God's timing. A seed takes time to germinate, and that is God's exact plan for our lives. His purpose within you will be fulfilled at the right time. However, you must set aside time for God and do his will (play your part)."*

In the darkest of times, God is using my book as a light for many people, and I am grateful that I get to contribute to the improvement and upward mobility of this generation and the generations to come through my book.

Becoming an author is a life-changing experience that allows you to contribute to service above self. It will enable you to take a slice of the world's marketplace and sell a product that could become the recipe that could change someone's life forever. My friend, you have a story to tell; make it your duty to write that book. Someone's change, hope, and future are in your mind. Give them a chance to succeed by writing your book. God bless.

Ontonio Dawson
Author- God's Seed for Success
Minister of Religion
Award Winning- Senior Cognitive Behavioural Psychotherapist
London, UK

"When I write, I give people access to their own emotions."
- Gord Downie

Writing has the power to enlarge your influence and reach many people in various ways:

1. **Global Reach:** Writing, especially in the digital age, allows your message to transcend geographical boundaries. Online platforms, blogs, and social media give you the platform and enable you to connect with people and share your books globally. Your words can be accessed and shared by individuals from different parts of the world.

2. **Timeless Impact:** Well-crafted written content has a timeless quality. Once published, it can continue to influence readers for an extended period. Books can be discovered and appreciated by new audiences years after their initial publication.

3. **Accessibility:** Writing makes your ideas, insights, and messages accessible to a wide audience. Readers can engage with your content at their own pace, allowing for a deeper understanding of complex topics. This accessibility is particularly valuable for individuals with diverse learning styles and preferences.

4. **Educational Value:** Whether you're sharing knowledge, experiences, or lessons learned, writing provides a structured and educational format. Readers can gain insights and information that contribute to their personal and intellectual growth.

5. **Building Authority:** Consistent and well-researched writing establishes you as an authority in your field. When people find valuable and reliable information in your content, they are more likely to trust your expertise. This can lead to increased influence and credibility.

6. **Engagement and Interaction:** Writing encourages engagement and interaction with your audience. Readers can respond through comments, social media, or direct messages, fostering a sense of community around your ideas. This interaction builds a stronger connection with your audience.

7. **Influence on Perspectives:** Through persuasive and thought-provoking writing, you can influence the perspectives and opinions of your readers. Your words have the potential to challenge assumptions,

inspire critical thinking, and open minds to new ideas.

8. **Inspiring Action:** Effective writing has the power to inspire action. Whether it's motivating people to make positive changes in their lives or encouraging them to contribute to a cause, your words can be a catalyst for meaningful action.

9. **Emotional Impact:** Writing allows you to convey emotions and connect with readers on a deeper level. Whether through storytelling, poetry, or personal reflections, you can evoke empathy and understanding, leaving a lasting emotional impact.

10. **Multiplying Impact Through Sharing:** Readers who resonate with your message are likely to share it with others. This word-of-mouth sharing can significantly amplify your reach. Social media platforms, in particular, provide a convenient way for readers to share books and other content with their networks.

11. **Leveraging Multiple Formats:** Beyond traditional writing, you can leverage multiple formats such as podcasts, videos, and visual

content. By adapting your written content into different formats, you cater to diverse preferences and learning styles, broadening your audience.

Writing is a powerful tool to extend your influence, share your message with a broader audience, and leave a positive and lasting impact on individuals worldwide. There is no limit to what you can achieve with doing the *write* thing. Whether you aim to educate, inspire, or initiate change, the written word remains a potent means of communication and can take your words and thoughts further than you could imagine.

"Any writer worth his salt writes to please himself. It's a self-exploratory operation that is endless."

- Harper Lee

Chapter 5

Writing a Book Helps to Raise Your Self-Esteem and Confidence

"Very few writers know what they are doing until they have done it."
- *Anne Lamott*

I've always had a healthy self-efficacy. I learned early not to allow people or circumstances to alter or diminish my value or self-worth. This served well in leading me on the path of becoming a motivational speaker and Christian life coach. Even with my thriving self-confidence, I didn't know writing a book could give me so much satisfaction, pride, and joy. Let's say this accomplishment elevated my self-esteem to unimaginable levels.

DO THE WRITE THING TODAY

When I held the first copy of my first book, I cried. It was a product of hard labor, sleepless nights, and creativity I didn't know I possessed. After authoring up, I felt like I could conquer the world. Not only did my self-value increase, but my respect barometer also recorded an unprecedented surge. The congratulations were endless, and the feedback was mind-blowing. My bookings increased, and people somehow found me more interesting.

Because my book was about the eagle, I was now seen as an eagle expert due to the extensive research I conducted to polish the message, which was evident in my book. Readers were especially impressed with how I wrote from a biblical perspective, and I was now a trusted source on certain biblical matters.

If your story carries elements of brokenness and shame, after writing and releasing it, you will feel the heavy burden lift and experience a new lease on life. Writing is like the Japanese art of "kintsugi;" it is the golden, silver, or platinum substance that is used to repair and mend the broken pieces of your life, making it a masterpiece and increasing your value and worth.

I could write extensively about how writing has impacted my mental health and inspired me to be a better person. Still, I will allow the testimony of Miguel, a Jamaican musician and firefighter, whose life was transformed after he dipped his toes in the pool of authorship, to share how the 3Ps rocketed his confidence:

"It is often said that 'he who wields a pen is mightier than he who wields a sword.' In reality, the veracity of this proverbial saying must be narrowed down to those parameters that define the skill level of either expert. In 1925, while incarcerated after attempting to seize power in Germany, Adolf Hitler, the infamous architect of World War 2, wrote his autobiography, *Mein Kampf* (My Struggle). What the dull sword of force had failed to do at first, Hitler, through his sharpened pen, was able to accomplish with relative ease. By injecting his poisonous ideologies into the minds of his compatriots, he was able to plunge an entire nation and, indeed, the whole world down a pathway of death and destruction.

Fortunately for the world, many well-intentioned authors have also left their indelible literary marks on the landscape of history. Through these portals, the reader is granted rare access to the minds of many great original thinkers and their experiences. Thus, they can better comprehend the nuanced peculiarities that characterize and distinguish every human.

The writing process has immensely impacted me, but I hasten to admit that it was not my original intention to become a writer, let alone an emotive expressionist. This outcome is largely my brother's fault. Derville had gone into independent publishing, and after having put a few titles on the market, he reached out to me and queried about a book I had only thought of doing but had yet to actively pursue - namely *Teach Yourself Piano*. I had many prospective students but little time to sacrifice for instructional sessions. So, I had been encouraged for some time before and had resolved to write a book.

After this initial publication, it was merely a matter of figuring out what to write about next. There can be so many dimensions to the intellectual range of any single individual that in any field of adequate exposure, a book could be derived. Of all the topics, however, I felt compelled to write about the flat earth theory - that is, to oppose it. I honestly didn't want to. This was such a cringy topic to align my reputation with. But I was being propelled by a power higher than myself. God required it.

Some Christians all over social media were mingling the flat earth theory with the message of the Gospel and spreading this idea through their very influential fervor and conviction. I was quite adept at geography and a diligent Bible scholar, so with this background, I was quite well-suited to deliver extensive commentary on the matter.

When I released *Flat Earth Fallacy*, I didn't even try to promote it. I was like a Jonah running away from my assigned daunting task of preaching to people who might just respond with ridicule. Flat Earth! Psshhh, you must have nothing to do. However, I received an extraordinary dose of confidence after my mom read and reviewed it. She had been diligently going through and had already gone to chapter 6 but had returned to chapter 5. When I asked why, what Mom said placed me on a pathway of ever-growing boldness and confidence as I wielded the power of my pen. She said, "I was enjoying your book so much I thought it was nearing the ending too quickly, so I went back to chapter 5."

DO THE WRITE THING TODAY

Up to this point, I still had no intention of distinguishing myself as a motivational or transformational writer. I was naturally inhibited - much too reserved to share details about my life.

But then, the real turn in confidence came. Frustrated and rather upset at certain marginalizations I had been compelled to endure, I finally exploded in a holy rant on social media. I had poured it all out on screen and simply pressed SEND—heedless of consequence and repercussion. Reader reactions were positive, however, and I was encouraged to write more about my experiences in a book. My friend, Hilette Virgo, invited me to contribute a 'Pit' experience to her next serial compilation, *Waiting in the Pit Volume 2*. I didn't immediately jump at the idea because I felt my own story had not arrived at a definitive landmark that particularly stood out as a positive terminal point.

Ideally, I hesitated to write pending the arrival of a real 'happily ever after' moment. But God had already supplied enough waymark experiences that could be related in their beneficial context. When Pit 2 came out, I was surprised at the interest my story generated. The unresolved tale of a mysteriously murdered wife and a grieving husband captivated the imagination.

At every step, the "write thing" revealed itself as a process worth engaging in, even if, after all that, I had ultimately decided not to publish. But in the words of the "Speed" villain, played by Dennis Hopper, "Bombs were made to explode." I needed to press send again.

Writing is a communicative process. In my case, it elicited a response from my audience, and when the desirable reaction came, I received it with gratitude. It returned vindication and release to my spirit and elevated me from the ground level of despair to new heights of confidence.

Having made myself vulnerable by revealing so much about my life, I feel no trepidation about what my blended audience of critics and supporters will think. It has been a most liberating process just penning those experiences. Each time I have gone over the script to edit, it has been a season of sniffles and welled-up tears - a true and real process of grieving that I had not been allowed to engage in freely.

Writing my story has helped me get over the trauma of loss - simply put, and while this process might not yet be complete, it has, for the most part, enabled me to find my true creative and productive self. I now freely indulge such lofty dreams, plans, hobbies, tasks, and projects that seem to have been locked away in a vault. And I live and speak in such expansive mental dimensions and frames of thought that can be exceeded by the eternal existence as promised by God. I highly recommend the "write thing" as a therapeutic tool for anyone who has been hurt, maligned, or misunderstood - and for anyone who simply needs to rant without interruption."

Miguel Lowe
Musician,
Composer,
Author

Writing a book can have several positive effects on self-esteem, contributing to personal growth and a sense of accomplishment. Here are ways in which writing a book can boost your self-esteem:

1. **Personal Achievement:** Completing a book is a significant personal achievement. The process of

conceiving, planning, and executing a long-form project demonstrates discipline, perseverance, and dedication. The sense of accomplishment from seeing a book through to completion can greatly enhance self-esteem.

2. **Expression of Creativity:** Writing allows you to express your creativity and unique perspective. Creating characters, developing plots, and crafting stories are creative endeavors that showcase your imagination. Seeing your creative ideas come to life on the pages of a book can instill a deep sense of pride, delight, and fulfillment.

3. **Mastery of Skills:** The act of writing a book involves honing various skills such as storytelling, character development, and narrative structure. As you refine these skills, you gain a sense of mastery and competence. When you have developed expertise in writing craft, your self-esteem will be significantly boosted.

4. **Sense of Purpose:** Having a goal and working towards it provides a sense of purpose. Writing a book gives you a clear objective and a project to

focus on. As you make progress and achieve milestones, you build confidence in your ability to set and attain meaningful goals.

5. **Overcoming Challenges:** Writing a book is not without challenges. Overcoming obstacles, whether writer's block, plot issues, or time constraints, builds resilience and self-efficacy. Successfully navigating these challenges will reinforce your belief in your ability to overcome difficulties.

6. **Validation and Recognition:** Receiving positive feedback and recognition for your writing, whether from beta readers, book coaches, editors, peers, or readers, can be a powerful source of validation. Knowing that your work has resonated with others contributes to a positive self-image.

7. **Increased Self-Understanding:** Writing often involves self-reflection and introspection. As you delve into your thoughts, experiences, and emotions, you gain a deeper understanding of yourself. This self-awareness can lead to greater self-acceptance and, consequently, improved self-esteem.

8. **Contribution to Knowledge:** Sharing your knowledge and insights through writing contributes to the collective body of human knowledge. Knowing that your ideas can impact and enrich the lives of others fosters a sense of significance and self-worth.

9. **Potential for Impact:** The belief that your words can influence and inspire others can be a powerful motivator. Knowing that your book has the potential to make a positive impact on readers can elevate your sense of purpose and self-esteem.

10. **Legacy Building:** Writing a book is a tangible representation of your thoughts, experiences, and wisdom. The idea that your words may endure, and influence future generations can be a source of pride and boost self-esteem.

Writing a book is a multifaceted journey that involves personal and creative growth. The process of creation, coupled with the tangible result of completing a book, can contribute significantly and enhance your sense of self-worth and self-esteem. Need a confidence boost? Do the *write* thing!

"When writing the story of your life, don't let anyone else hold the pen."

- Harley Davidson

Chapter 6

Write Because Your Story is Unique

"I now see how owning your story and loving ourselves through that process is the bravest thing that we will ever do."
- **Brene Brown**

No two people have the same story. In my experience as a book coach and indie publisher, many prospective clients query whether their story or message is worth writing. They fear their testimony or story won't be exciting or impactful enough or that many others may have had similar experiences; hence, it is not worth writing or reading.

My answer has always been and will forever be a resounding YES! Like a fingerprint or iris, your story is unique; no one has the same story as yours. Even if your experiences are like other people's, your story, which encapsulates your experiences, mindset, and character, combined with your writing style and tone, makes your story exceptionally unique.

As an editor, I am often tempted to declare that I have seen and read it all after poring over hundreds of stories and manuscripts. God, however, has a gentle and unique way of humbling me by sending the next manuscript. There are always elements and details in the next story that I have never seen before.

Consequently, I have come to the indisputable conclusion that there is always another space on the shelves of a reader's heart and mind for one more book, yours.

Shasta, a beautiful Dominican, had fears that her story would not be widely accepted, especially in the Christian community, because of its nature. She feared how the world would perceive her after she released a secret she had kept that had haunted her for years. After sharing, she realized that God handpicked her to be the conduit through which a message of hope was delivered to a host of people who suffered silently. Not only was her calling unique, but she discovered how distinctive her writing style and storyline were after the writing process. This revelation silenced her fears, boosted her confidence, and gave her a new outlook on her purpose and ministry.

She shares her testimony:

"Paul wrote in the book of Romans chapter 8, "All things work together for good to them that love God."

When someone hurts you, it is hard to imagine the good that can come from it. As a matter of fact, Paul's writings did not soothe the hurt that happened to me. Instead, they magnified my question: how can good come from hurt? You see, hurt blurs reality; it makes a mess of the truth and appears to honor lies.

My hurt was childhood sexual trauma. The reality that my home was a safe place was blurred because a family member violated it. The truth of a girl growing up to be beautiful and adventurous was messed up with the thoughts that unwanted sexual attraction was to be my scarlet letter, and that real adventure comes from multiple sexual partners. The lies that were honored were that boys don't get hurt, that a sexual relationship with a female is safer, and I must have done something to attract these sexual traumas. These mendacities plagued me for years.

Then, a friend of mine received her catharsis from writing. She wanted me to experience that same release. It is interesting how three p's relieved years of plagues and pressure. They are prayers, a pen and paper. Through prayers, the Holy Spirit prepared me to be ready to move past my past. Through the ink of a pen, the hurt and shame were pulled from the cells and sinews of my body that stored them, and through the paper, a safe space was created to capture the ugliness and transform it into a unique and beautiful work of art that has blessed numerous souls.

In chapter 4 of the book named in his honor, John recounts the woman's encounter at the well with the Messiah. She also experienced pain, hurt, and shame. Her sex appeal was the attraction of men and the scorn of women. But meeting Christ changed her past, her now, and her future. I resonated with her. I, too, met Christ, and my past received clarity, I now received healing, and my future will help to heal others who share similar childhood trauma as myself. Through the powerful potency of the 3Ps, I learned to embrace my story as one that is unique with restorative power. Christ used the mess of my past to create something beautiful that can be a catalyst of healing and restoration to many.

Christ knows our every smile and every sorrow. Through His love and grace, every crevice of pain receives light, healing, and transformation. Writing is the vehicle that transported me from shame to esteem and highlighted my authenticity. The best part is that I didn't need a license to drive; all I needed was to place one hand in Christ's and use the other to work my favorite pen.

The 3Ps are your treasure chest. I now confer the key to you. Let prayer, pen, and paper drive you to your place of power and authenticity. I look forward to reading your story."

Shasta Green
Counselor
Occupational Therapist

Your story or testimony is unique because it is a personal story shaped by your individual experiences, perspectives, and journey. Several factors contribute to the uniqueness of your story:

1. **Personal Experiences:** Your life experiences, whether challenging or uplifting, form the foundation of your story. No one else has lived through the exact combination of events, relationships, and circumstances that you have.

2. **Perspective:** Your viewpoint and interpretation of events are entirely yours. Your unique perspective is influenced by your background, culture, values, and beliefs. This distinct lens shapes how you perceive and narrate your story.

3. **Resilience and Growth:** Your story may include instances of resilience, overcoming adversity, and personal growth. The challenges you've faced and the lessons you've learned contribute to the distinctive narrative of your journey that no one else has.

4. **Individual Choices and Decisions:** The choices you've made, both significant and mundane, have led you down a particular path. These decisions, influenced by your personality and circumstances, make your story unlike anyone else's.

5. **Interpersonal Relationships:** The relationships you've formed, whether with family, friends, or significant others, play a crucial role in your story. The dynamics and nuances of these relationships add depth and uniqueness to your narrative.

6. **Cultural and Environmental Context:** The cultural and environmental context in which you've lived shapes your story. Your upbringing, the places you've lived, and the cultural influences around you contribute to the distinctive elements of your narrative.

7. **Achievements and Milestones:** Your accomplishments, milestones, and moments of success are part of your story. Whether big or small, these achievements are unique to your journey and contribute to the overall narrative.

8. **Challenges and Setbacks:** The challenges you've encountered and setbacks you've faced are inherent to your story. How you've navigated through difficulties and what you've learned from setbacks are integral components of your unique narrative.

9. **Character Traits and Personality:** Your character traits, strengths, weaknesses, and personality quirks are woven into your story. These elements contribute to the authenticity and distinctiveness of your narrative.

10. **Evolution Over Time:** Your story is not static; it evolves. The person you were in the past, your present self, and your aspirations for the future contribute to the dynamic and ever-changing nature of your unique story.

Embracing the uniqueness of your story involves recognizing and celebrating the individuality of your experiences. By sharing your authentic narrative, you offer a perspective that can resonate with and inspire others who may find similarities or lessons in your journey.

"When you speak, your words echo across the room. When you write, your words echo across the ages."

– Chicken Soup for the Writers Soul author Bud Gardner

Chapter 7

Write to Leave a Legacy

> *"Let this be recorded for a generation to come, so that a people yet to be created may praise the LORD:"*
> *(Psalm 102:18 NLT)*

A book is a powerful three-way bridge that connects the past with the present and the present to the future. Every day, we benefit from the legacy of someone who no longer walks this earth through their books. All the Bible authors left the succeeding generations a legacy, from the first script by Moses to the last written by John on an island off the coast of Turkey around 95 A.D.

John benefitted from the Old Testament writers' legacy, whose works span over four thousand years. God ensured that through time, His words were preserved through scrolls and later transferred to papyrus or parchment that were folded and stitched into a codex. Several centuries later, the first printing of books started in China. Then, in the 1450s, the first Bible was printed, and countless generations later, we are still feasting on this legacy.

God preserved this beautiful vestige, so you and I may benefit from the testimonies of the past and have a clear direction for the future. Speaking of direction, I explained how a book can be used as a COMPASS for your ministry in another book I wrote on this inexhaustive subject of writing titled *Booked for Ministry*. Books carry so much value, possess such transformative power, and have the propensity, much like a compass, to direct us to the past to see how far we've come. It also helps us to navigate the terrains of the present and the future. One of my most significant accomplishments as a ghostwriter is writing a memoir on behalf of a 96-year-old man. Although he could not read, this man possessed such wisdom that I was too happy to sit at his feet as I was transformed several decades back in time.

His chief purpose for writing was to leave a legacy for his family. So much was revealed through this expedition that his children are beyond grateful that he insisted on getting his story recorded. This book brought such clarity to the family, who didn't realize that they had carried several unanswered questions over the years. Not only were questions answered, but they were also able to trace certain traits and understand themselves and their families better from the elements revealed. At the end of publishing, a cathartic sigh was released from this near centurion, and his family realized that a legacy of priceless value had been gifted to them. His daughter, Janet Fider, shares:

"My father, Robert Nicholson, got his book, Bobby, *the Mad Mint Man,* detailing his life story from childhood to adulthood, written at the ripe age of 96. This book has brought him immense joy and lit up the life of a man who had this burning desire and vision to leave his story behind as a legacy. I am happy I could make this a reality at this point in his life.

He is so proud of his accomplishment that he tells everyone about his book. He takes the book and his flyers everywhere and shows them to all the people he meets. He takes them to church and on his doctor's visits.

Everyone in the family is happy for him, knowing that he lived his desire to leave a legacy for his children, grandchildren, and great-grandchildren. We are especially thrilled that he got to tell his story. No one could have captured it the way he did in sharing the details and the sacred moments, some of which he had never mentioned to anyone.

We learned so much about him from his book. Many of the events detailed are new information to us, and as we read, we identify patterns, trends, and character traits that all of us, as his children and even the grandchildren, possess that came directly from him. For example, I grew up seeing my dad hosting annual dance events; I didn't know his father did the same thing. Additionally, for years, I watched my nephews with a preference for white sneakers. I know it's not a pop trend because I observe other young people in the community wearing bright colors and different styles. Through the book, I learned that my father had that same preference for white casual footwear as a youth. I also realized that I got my resilient spirit from him.

Many times, an heirloom is only passed on to one child. Leaving a book as a legacy is profound because all his children, grandchildren, and great-grandchildren can access copies, and even his church and community friends. This legacy can be distributed to millions. There is no limit to its reach. His story will never be erased from history and passed on to many generations.

My father's book is not just a memoir; it has great historical and educational value, especially for the small community in Jamaica where he resides. He pays tribute to people who contributed to the community's development and shares events worth knowing about.

I can't express enough how grateful and blessed we are to have tangible documentation of his life written in his voice. When you read it, you can hear his voice as if he is speaking directly to you. We know we will not always have him around, but we are comforted that after he is gone, we will have these great memories preserved through his book as a reminder of his extraordinary life.

I recommend that every family invest in documenting the lives of their loved ones as a legacy and a means of honoring their loved ones. My dad did the right thing in insisting that his life's story be written, and I am happy we supported his dream and made it happen.

Hilette Virgo was our ghostwriter, and she did an exceptional job capturing his tone and voice. If you or someone you know has an interesting story but doesn't know how to write it, consider doing the writing thing and hiring a ghostwriter. It's worth the investment. Get that legacy out of your system for future generations to benefit from."

Janet Fider

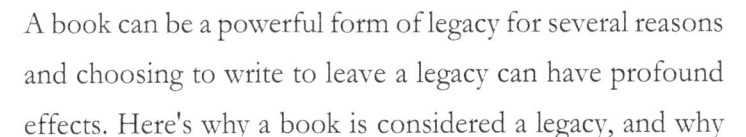

A book can be a powerful form of legacy for several reasons and choosing to write to leave a legacy can have profound effects. Here's why a book is considered a legacy, and why individuals may choose to write to leave a lasting impact:

1. **Permanence and Timelessness:** A book endures through time, often outliving its author. It becomes a tangible representation of the author's thoughts, experiences, and wisdom. Unlike other forms of communication, books have the potential to remain relevant across generations.

2. **Sharing Knowledge and Wisdom:** Writing a book allows you to share your accumulated

knowledge, insights, and life lessons with a wide audience. It becomes a repository of wisdom that can guide, inspire, and educate others, including future generations.

3. **Inspiration for Others:** A well-crafted book can serve as a source of inspiration for readers. Whether it's a memoir, self-help book, or fiction with meaningful themes, your words can motivate others to overcome challenges, pursue their dreams, or simply view life from a different perspective.

4. **Preserving Personal Stories:** Your personal stories, anecdotes, and experiences can be preserved for posterity. Family members, friends, and future generations can gain a deeper understanding of your life, values, and the context in which you lived.

5. **Contribution to Knowledge and Culture:** Non-fiction books, especially those in areas like history, science, or philosophy, contribute to the collective knowledge and cultural heritage of humanity. They become part of a broader conversation that transcends individual lifetimes.

6. **Impact on Society:** Books have the power to shape minds and influence societal norms. By writing about topics that matter to you, you can contribute to positive change, challenge existing perspectives, and advocate for causes important to you.

7. **Legacy of Creativity:** For those who express themselves through fiction, poetry, or creative works, a book is a tangible representation of artistic expression. It allows you to leave behind a legacy of creativity that can be appreciated by others who share a love for the arts.

8. **Connecting with Future Generations:** Writing a book provides a means of connecting with individuals who may come into existence long after your time. It allows you to communicate with, inspire, and influence people who might not have had the opportunity to know you personally.

9. **Immortality of Ideas:** Ideas, philosophies, and perspectives expressed in a book can outlive the author, creating a form of intellectual immortality. Your ideas continue to exist and resonate,

influencing those who encounter them in the future.

10. **Fulfillment and Legacy Building:** For many authors, the act of writing and leaving behind a tangible legacy brings a sense of fulfillment. It's a way of making a lasting mark on the world and leaving something meaningful for others to discover.

Writing to leave a legacy is a conscious decision to make a lasting impact on the world. Whether it's through sharing personal stories, imparting knowledge, or inspiring others, the written word has the potential to create a legacy that extends far beyond the author's lifetime.

"The graveyard is the richest place on Earth because it is here that you will find all the hopes and dreams that were never fulfilled, the books that were never written…"

Conclusion

> *"Writing is a calling, not a choice."*
> *- Isabel Allende*

Writing is one of life's most noble, elevating, liberating, and gratifying feats. Writing for leisure and emptying one's mind through avenues of journaling can prove therapeutic. However, penning a work to publish through the channel of a book is a life-altering aspiration.

The benefits of writing are endless. Penning your story to access healing, honor God, inspire and save a soul, enlarge your scope of influence, share your unique story, boost your self-worth, and leave a legacy are only a few reasons you should share your story and message with the world. Yet, they are enough to propel you to do the *write* thing today!

Having gotten this far, I know any form of self-doubt, fear, or insecurity has evaporated. Congratulations on your decision to do the *write* thing today. There is no better time to start than now. Here are three beautiful quotes that should give you the impetus to get going.

"The scariest moment is always just before you start."
- Stephen King

"Start writing, no matter what. The water does not flow until the faucet is turned on."
- Louis L'Amour

"There is something delicious about writing the first words of a story. You never quite know where they'll take you."
- Beatrix Potter

About the Author

*B*estselling author, editor, ghostwriter, poet, songwriter, singer, independent publisher, book coach, and motivational speaker, Hilette Virgo is known as the "Book Doula." She writes, edits, and publishes faith-based books.

She has authored seven books and is the visionary for the three books in the *Waiting in the Pit* series. With her expertise in writing, editing, and coaching, she gently comforts, supports, and reassures her clients as they birth their books.

She is the CEO of twin companies Great-Nest Publishing and Great-Nest Coaching Academy, whose mantra is, "Tap into your Great-nest, soar into your GREATNESS."

Hilette is an avid Christian committed to inspiring and serving others. She loves the Lord fiercely and has a calling and mission to encourage everyone she meets, one spoken and written word at a time.

Other books authored by Hilette Virgo:

- Activating Her Eagle Instincts
- Evoking Your Divine Dove
- Waiting in the Pit: Stories of Renewal, Deliverance and God's Nurturing Care
- Waiting in the Pit: Testimonies of Tests, Tears, Trials, and Triumphs
- Waiting in the Pit: Stories of Brokenness, Benevolence, Blessings, and Breakthroughs
- Booked for Ministry
- From Manuscript to Missions and Ministry

Upcoming Books

- Spurring Your Sparrow Spirit
- Purple, Pearls and Promises
- Jars, Net, Bed and Breakfast
- I Am: My Knight in Shining Armor
- Dining with Mary and Elizabeth

Made in the USA
Columbia, SC
27 July 2024